LINUS
The Magician

BY
ROSALIE BARKER

HARBOR
HOUSE (West)
PUBLISHERS

© 1993 Rosalie Barker, Santa Barbara, CA 93103
All rights reserved.

ISBN
1-879560-28-2

Library of Congress Catalog Card Number
93-79957

No part of this book may be copied or transmitted by any method, including fax, computer, or by any other printed, electronic or broadcast medium, without the express permission of the Publisher.

Manufactured in the United States of America

Harbor House (West) Publishers, Inc.
Drawer 599, Summerland, CA 93067

10 9 8 7 6 5 4 3 2 1

My special thanks to Soozie Bing
for her contribution to this book.

Hi!
MY NAME IS
LINUS…
I'm called that
Because
I'm really just a line,
But
I can do
many magical
THINGS.

Lines can do many magical things!
I can use my powers to change my **WIDTH.** If I go
on a diet, I can be THIN, THIN, **THIN!**
Or, I can easily inflate myself to get FAT, FAT, **FAT!**

I can also magically change my **LENGTH**.
As you can see, I can stretch myself out and be **TALL**
or I can shrink myself to become very **SHORT**.

A line that goes straight up and down is called a **VERTICAL** line. When I stand up straight and tall, I am like a tree, VERTICAL and strong.

A line that lies down is called a **HORIZONTAL** line. The word 'HORIZONTAL' comes from the word **'HORIZON'**. The HORIZON is the long, flat line where earth meets sky. A HORIZONTAL line is restful.

A slanting line is called a **DIAGONAL**.
DIAGONAL lines can show energy and motion.
When I lean and stretch into a DIAGONAL,
I appear to be moving very fast.

CURVED lines can also show movement. The CURVED lines make this giant wave look as though it will crash any minute!

If I push two DIAGONAL lines against each other, I create a feeling of **TENSION**. TENSION is not a restful feeling. Do these two lines look mad at each other? TENSION will do that.

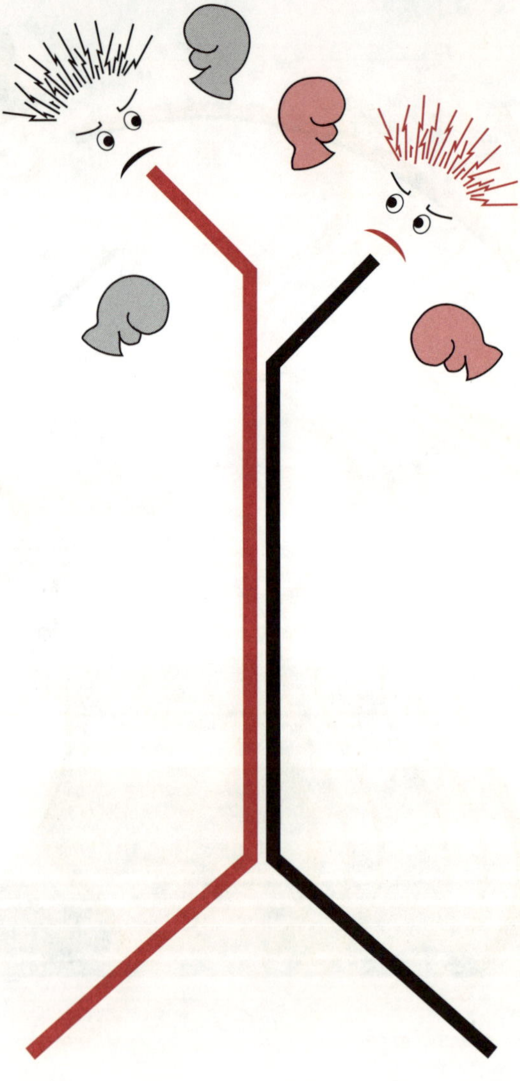

When I wiggle back and forth, I make **WAVY** lines.
Don't these lines look like they're dancing?

Just by **POINTING** to something
I can catch your attention.

SUPER SALE!

Did you know that we show how we **FEEL** by the lines on our faces?

One of my famous magic tricks is to **ENCLOSE SPACE** and make you see shapes and objects.

LINUS

I can make lots of different shapes. When I go round and round I can make a **CIRCLE**!

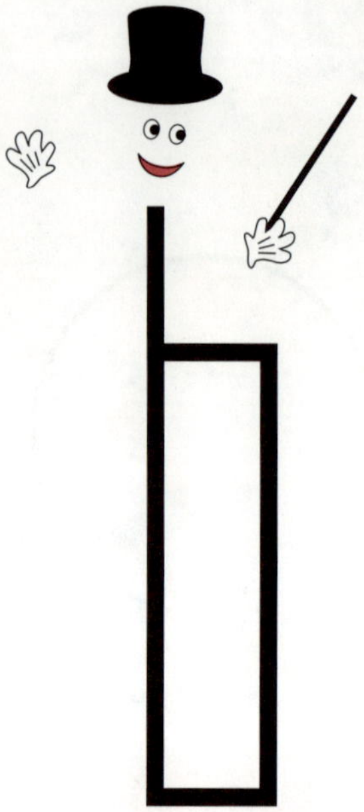

When I bend four ways, I become a **SQUARE** or **RECTANGLE**.

Three bends . . . and I'm a **TRIANGLE**.

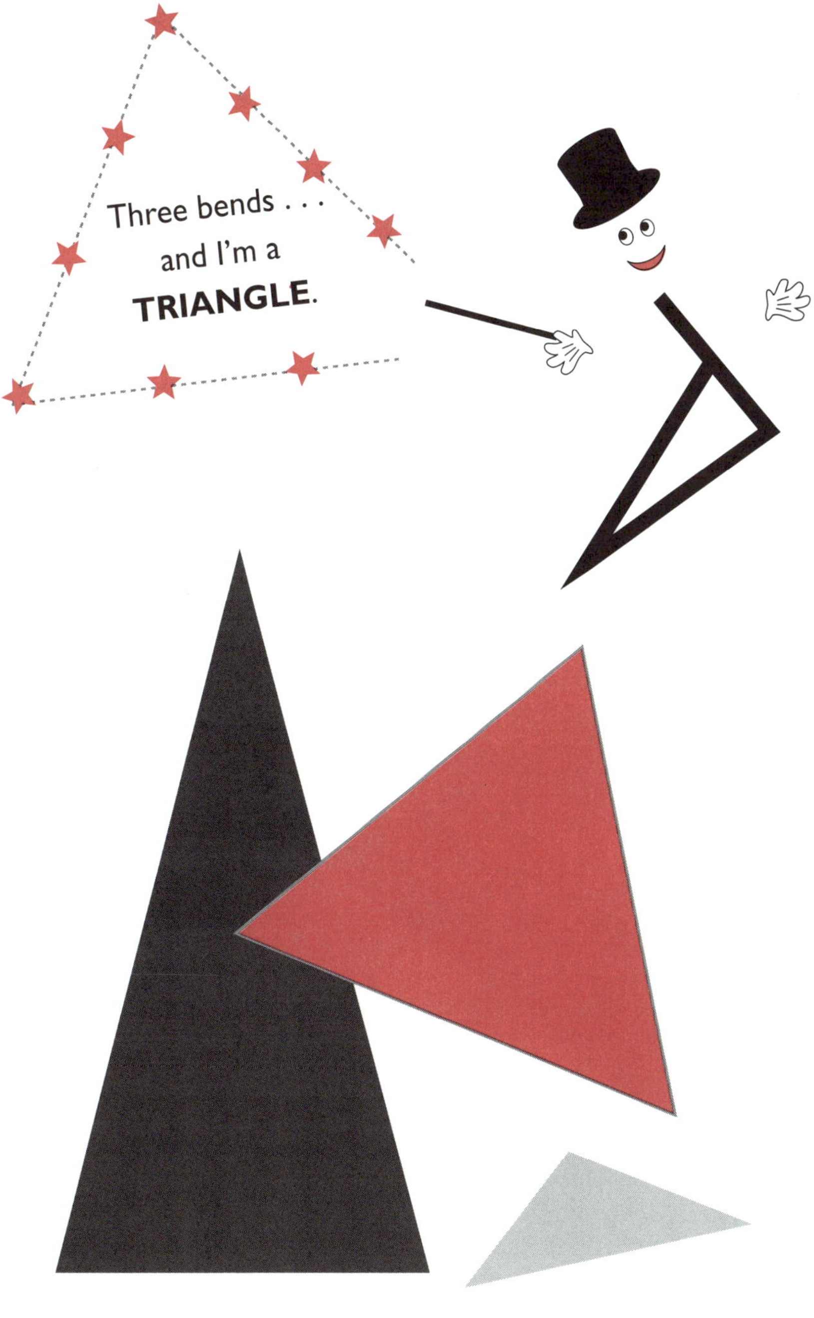

Did you know that I look SMALLER as I go further away? See the HORIZON in this picture? This is a way to show **DISTANCE**.

I can fool you into thinking I am different LENGTHS.
Which of me is **LONGER** here?
Measure both lines to see if you guessed right.

Here's another way I can **FOOL YOU**.
In this picture do you see a goblet—or do you see two people looking at each other? Ha, ha!

Some people may say,
"YOU'RE NOTHING BUT A LINE!"
But I am the world's **GREATEST MAGICIAN**
and I'm proud of what I am BECAUSE . . .

WITHOUT ME, YOU WOULD SEE

NOTHING!

QUIZ!
How many of my different shapes can you find in the picture below?

Now it's your turn to have Linus do what you'd like him to do. Draw him doing your favorite thing. If you'll send your drawing to Linus, he'll send you an autographed picture to hang on your wall! Send your pictures to: Linus the Magician, c/o Harbor House (West) Publishers, Drawer 599, Summerland, California 93067.

Watch for the future adventures of Linus—
who can say what he'll be doing next!